We Are Meaningful

Kristen Holland

BookLeaf
Publishing

Presentation by *BookLeaf Publishing*

Web: www.bookleafpub.com

E-mail: info@bookleafpub.com

ISBN: 978-93-95755-34-4

First edition 2022

To all people feeling lonely, scared, lost, hurt, lovelorn, forsaken, disappointed, and in general feeling different from what they feel they should have been. Essentially, this is for everyone.

And for the fairies: they never stopped believing in me and I never stopped believing in them.

ACKNOWLEDGEMENT

Thank you to my comrades in poetic expression, Ceren and Sierra. Your encouragement gave me confidence that my poems were worth sharing.

untitled

I am alone again…
And I'm not alone.
Every beautiful moment keeps me company
In the shadows of lost things.

I find them sometimes,
Hiding in my room and thoughts,
Waiting to be recognized.
I try my best, but memory fades and changes,
Until the blank breath of death blows them
away.

I am one of them:
Unfound, unseen, unacknowledged,
Alone.
But not alone.
Will you save us?

Into the Night

I have dreams
Of dancing flames and drum beats
And passion flying on the wind.
Of you and me, and a willow tree
Bound in everlasting night.

We fly between the light and darkness
Swirling together in a never-ending song
Of Earth and Air, and Fire and Water,
Always opposing yet in perfect harmony.
Never ceasing, slowing, or tiring.

We are them, and they are us,
Innocently tantalizing.
The song goes on long after I awake,
My own heartbeat constantly reminding me
Of what it feels like to be alive.

Heartbeat

3

Do you ever notice how we complain about the
most mundane things?
Is it that we truly find that much wrong with our
world,
Or do we just like the sound of our own voices
that much?
I honestly don't know which of these answers I'd
prefer.

Maybe we've talked about and said everything
there is to say
And we complain to have something to say in
the silence that surrounds us...
But truth be told, I live for those moments when
all other sounds are suspended
And I can hear the heartbeat of the world again.

Together

I miss you and the way we could talk about
anything:
Our hopes, our dreams. Our fears, our pain…
We built a world for ourselves in the land of
"when we"
And never dared to question it.
We dreamed of things too big for us,
But that was why we dreamed of them together.

Terrain of My Bedsheets

5

I am once again lost in the terrain of my
bedsheets,
The core to plates of blankets spreading over
me.
I map out the world I have unexpectedly created,
Charting mountains, lakes, valleys, and
heartbreaks.
I move and the terrain changes, never to be the
same again.
It's still beautiful, just different.
And I'm once again lost in the terrain of my
bedsheets,
Not to be found until morning.

University

I feel like I spun straw into gold only to have an
even poorer future than before.
I was seduced by the status and prestige,
Being told things like "the purpose of life is to
convert energy into beauty" and "only with
questions is there a possibility for answers."
But they kept us half-awake to mold our
unobjecting minds into a perfect replica of
theirs,
Except they gave us their faults too.
They said they know so much but all they ever
taught me is how to be fast and cut corners.
Nothing I did should have been good enough,
But I found myself content with half-assed
efforts
And was too consumed with just getting through
it all to care.
I traded in my heroes for ghosts and wasted my
youth,
Holding onto memories that mean nothing to
anyone but me now.
How did I get this far?
My head is so full that it's empty,
And all I really know is that spinning straw into
gold isn't as profitable as you would think.

Not an Apology

I try so hard to live up to your standards,
But it's never good enough.
You put me in a dictionary as if I could be defined or
compared to something more lasting than I am.
But then so were you.
You hold people up to the same standards that you
were held against and hate,
Desexualizing flowers to make yourself seem more
virtuous.
We all do it.
We all allowed the boxes to grow in around us until it
was us who was in the box,
All nice and neat for the next generation to be judged
against.
I am by no means perfect or flawless,
But you will either hide my demons and call me saint
Or put them on display and call me sinner,
Anything to make the future seem more certain than
it is
And the past more educational than it was.

I know I'm not good at being what people want me to
be,
But I don't know how not to be me.

Reflections

People don't know the back of their own hands
until they see them in a mirror,
Becoming pirates to themselves every time they
take a picture,
Fracturing with each flash of the camera.
They tell themselves they lived out their lives in
childhood,
With memories to last a lifetime so they have
something to smile back on when all their pieces
are auctioned off.
Yet adults are surprised when children act like
children because they've forgotten what it's like.
They run, run, run, as fast as they can
Because they can't catch their words… but
everyone else can.
Their stories are no longer theirs,
And when our stories replace our reality we
question what the hell we're living in,
If you can call it living,
Wondering how our lives are more cliché when
written than the stories we create.

Moments With You

I have been uncommonly lucky to have lived a full life,
…Or to have been easily captured by beauty.
Although those little victories so often seem overshadowed by the great disappointments.
Success, however, is not just finding those moments of happiness,
But in finding the courage to move on when they are gone.
I failed when I tried to keep you with me,
Even if it was just your smell I held.
See, you built my life around me with your hugs and smiles,
Like you were trying to give me a lifetime of memories in the time we had left.

I wish I could keep you forever,
But death is not a pawn to be used for your own benefit,
It is the Queen and the whole board and game is run by it.
I would ask for more time but time is precariously balanced
And if it falls, it would fall on us.

Although you told me "ashes to ashes, and dust
to dust,"
You never mentioned that your bones would
crumble too.
So I'll be singing lullabies at graves in case the
angels don't come in time,
Until the moment your breath is taken away.

Post-Op

I envy people who know who they are.
Too often I feel like I'm piecing myself together,
Line for line in a helter-skelter poem,
Trying to find myself in the words I have written
or the books I have read.
But I'm not there. Not all of me.
I'm in my photographs too, and my clothes,
And in a million other small things that I
normally take for granted.
But here, away from all of me, I feel threatened
with all the inadequacies I could become,
Realizing that I can cry over books, and I can
cry over movies,
But I just can't cry over real life.

Recovery

I can't feel pain until my anger is gone,
Anger at myself for not remembering.
I want to hit myself in an attempt to jolt my
memory back,
Fighting to keep a conversation in mind but
seeing it slip away
With every little distraction or stray thought.

I try to convince myself when it's bad that it was
worse before,
But I always end up hurting anyway.
I try to explain it to people, but I can never
explain it just right,
And then I stutter and stumble over my words
and concede defeat to my own body.
Will this nightmare ever end?

Unknown

13

To know the contours of my own head,
Mapping out every crater and ridge
Like the explorers of the moon...
It is just as unknown to me,
Holding just as many secrets,
And is just as fascinating and scary.
I too wonder which crater will be my last.

What If?

I wish I could be someone else,
Someone who could cry because they've been
strong for too long.
But it's hard to trust people when I'm used to
doing things on my own.
So I keep my heart in a cage, away from all the
hurt,
But it was trapped in loneliness as well.
Where is the love when you need it the most?

I wanted to tell you but I was too afraid of the
look you might give me
…Or at least that's what I tell myself.
I've heard that you can't wait for your life to
begin, you just have to start living it now,
But the "what ifs" of this world are the hardest
of all to bear because they are the embodiment
of our uncertainty.

What if this isn't all over?
What if I'm never the same?
What if you don't feel the same way about me?
What if?

Every so often I catch my reflection and wonder
why I'm not in that world with you
Where we hold each other as we cry for a
different kind of love.

Thank You

You let me forget, just for a bit,
You let me be just the girl that you talked to.
You brushed my worries and fears aside like
they were nothing,
Like they were smaller than you, and me, and
everything that happened that night.
And you made me believe they could be.

People wake without waking, only knowing that
their dreams aren't true and never questioning
why,
But I would gladly keep you as a dream if it
allowed me to keep feeling the way I felt with
you.
After all, dreams never die, they just move on to
a stronger heart.
So when the memory of you is gone and there's
nothing left on Earth,
We'll light ourselves on fire just so we can
watch the world burn.

Lost and Found

The terrain of your body is branded into my
skin,
Discovered inch by inch with my fingertips,
Recorded in detail in the vault of my mind.
The mountains and valleys of your muscles,
The ebb and flow of your heartbeat,
Are all mapped out in perfect memory with
perfect clarity.
But I got lost in you anyway.

You drew me in deeper with every curve of your
being
Until I no longer wanted to know the way back.
I may have found you, only to be lost,
But I could never regret knowing you, come
what may.
If I am lost, I'm glad it was in you,
And you can always find me in the sunset,
And the stars that we call home.

Winter With You

We only try to capture moments of time when
we start to see them slipping away,
And I hate waking up and realizing I am one day
further gone.
My precious time has slipped away while I slept
And I still never told you what I needed to.
When I leave I find myself hoping to smell you
on my skin,
Looking for any connection to you so it doesn't
seem so permanent,
Hating that I can't trust people when they say it
won't be.

I don't know exactly what I feel,
But I wish I had time to figure it out with you.
Deep down I know that after winter there is
always spring,
But this winter with you will never seem long
enough in my memory.

Beau

When all is said and done
We will be left with silence and blank stares.
Maybe it was you I was drawing on the pages,
Quietly waiting and watching me for this
moment.
Did you see it coming?
Because I should have.
Looking back I could read between the lines
And hear what I couldn't say:
I needed you.
I will always be thankful to you for being there,
But I want to live, not just survive.
And I know in your heart that you want that too.
I want to thank you for everything, even if you
don't want to hear it.
And I hope that someday you will hear these
words
Instead of just "good-bye."

Half-Finished Picture

You and I were only ever a half-finished picture,
Never together long enough for pictures or
opinions to fully develop.
Sometimes I wonder what would have happened
if we only sat still long enough.
Would we have liked the picture we became?

I think of you often, not because you were my
first love,
But because you were the first one to love me
back,
Even if you never said it.
I don't think we would have worked,
But we did make a beautiful half-finished
picture.

Shattered

You broke my heart,
Over and over again.
You encouraged me to believe in you,
But then you turned out just like all the others.
I wanted to have some distance,
I knew that all loves were the same.
But then I paused for a second and that distance got
shorter
And next thing I knew…
You.

I put so much faith in you,
More than you ever knew or could guess.
Building you up in my mind until the only way
forward for you was down.
I couldn't help it,
And neither could you;
We were both just trying to find a way to work.
Each little crack sent a spiderweb through us
Until we became unrecognizable in the fragmentation
of our faults.

Yet I still can't help but find beauty in the pieces of
you,
Can't teach myself to hate it.
Love knows no boundaries,
Not even the jagged edges of a broken heart.

Moments

Light has the ability to transform the world,
Not to make it more beautiful, but to turn it into
something new
So that we may experience the beauty again.
Every moment is the only moment in which a
certain thing will look the way it does.
Once that moment is gone it is lost forever.
The Sun will never shine exactly the same way
on exactly the same spot,
Even if that spot had the misfortune of never
changing.
But that is part of the beauty and magic:
A moment is only for a moment, and then it is
gone.
They will not go down in history like the
carnage of a war or the fall of an empire,
But each image is etched into my being
And will live with me in my eternity.

For Everyone

It can sometimes seem that life is shitty,
That it throws at you more than you can bear.
But being as young as we are and having all our
bad happen now is not such a bad thing.
We learn to deal with the worst first
So everything later seems easier.
We have only lived a third of our lives
So let us enjoy the pie that we have left
And not dwell on the pain of our past.

Don't say we are forever a never and never a
forever,
But that sometimes you have to stir up some shit
before you can find what you're looking for.
So let us stir up the shit that life hands us and
find that we are meaningful,
And make those moments when our lives seem
to crumble
Turn into something good instead of bad.
It's the small moments, those little victories, that
make an eternity worth living in,
And I am so glad I got at least one moment with
you.